Fingerprint Wizards

The Secrets of Forensic Science

Ross Piper

Produced for A & C Black by

MONKEY PUZZLE MEDIA LTD
Monkey Puzzle Media Ltd
The Rectory, Eyke, Woodbridge
Suffolk IP12 2QW, UK

Published by A & C Black Publishers Limited
38 Soho Square, London W1D 3HB

First published 2008
Copyright © 2008 A & C Black Publishers Limited

ISBN 978-1-4081-0021-9 (hardback)
ISBN 978-1-4081-0099-8 (paperback)

A CIP catalogue record for this book is available
from the British Library.

Editor: Cath Senker
Design: Mayer Media Ltd
Picture research: Shelley Noronha and Lynda Lines
Series consultant: Jane Turner

This book is produced using paper that is made
from wood grown in managed, sustainable forests.
It is natural, renewable and recyclable. The logging
and manufacturing processes conform to the
environmental regulations of the country of origin.

Printed in China by C & C Offset Printing Co., Ltd

Picture acknowledgements
Alamy p. 18 right (Louise Murray); Corbis pp. 6 (Bill
Fritsch/Brand X), 19 (Jeremy Horner), 26 (Steve
Klaver); Georgia Bureau of Investigation p. 24;
Getty Images pp. 5 (Patti McConville), 7, 9 (AFP), 15
(AFP), 28 bottom (AFP), 29; iforensic.com p. 28 top;
Rex Features p. 17 (Denis Closen); Science Photo
Library pp. 1 (Paul Rapson), 4 (Paul Rapson), 8 (Tek
Image), 10 (Paul Rapson), 11 (Alfred Pasieka), 12 right
(Gustoimages), 13 (Alfred Pasieka), 14 (Volker Steger/
Peter Arnold Inc), 16 (Mauro Fermariello), 18 left (Jim
Varney), 21 (Philippe Psaila), 22 (Andrew Lambert), 23
(Geoff Tompkinson), 25 (Mauro Fermariello); Topfoto
pp. 20 (Photonews), 27 (Photonews). Artwork on
p. 12 left by Tim Mayer.

The front cover shows computer artwork of a
glowing human handprint (Science Photo Library/
Alfred Pasieka).

Every effort has been made to contact copyright
holders of material reproduced in this book. Any
omissions will be rectified in subsequent printings if
notice is given to the publishers.

CONTENTS

Abbreviations **m** stands for metres · **ft** stands for feet · **cm** stands for centimetres
in stands for inches

Fantastic forensics

At first, some crimes look impossible to solve. Fortunately, there is a special kind of investigator who helps the police to find clues that ordinary people would never see. This investigator is called a forensic expert.

Forensics is the use of science to help solve crimes. Forensic experts are among the first people at a crime scene. They hunt for evidence and carefully take it back to the forensic science laboratory. They try to work out what happened and help to trace the criminals.

Evidence everywhere

Evidence can be a tiny fibre of clothing, a piece of paper left at the crime scene or even a single strand of hair.

Every piece of evidence is placed in a separate plastic evidence bag.

Date of Manufacture 01.04

B 197267

EVIDENCE BAG

Write Using Ball Point Pen

(Continuity)

Name/Rank/No. (Block Letters)

Police Force ....

Identification Ref. No. ....

Court Exhibit No. ....

Signed ....

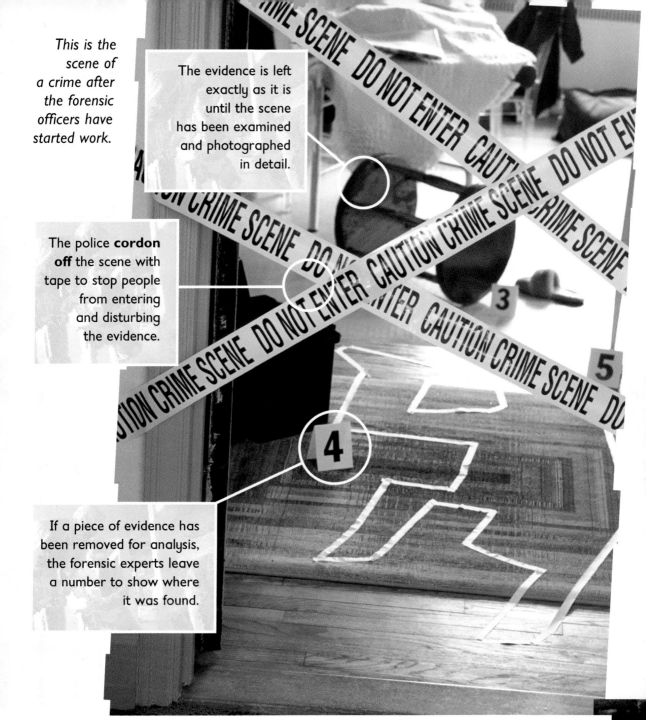

This is the scene of a crime after the forensic officers have started work.

The evidence is left exactly as it is until the scene has been examined and photographed in detail.

The police **cordon off** the scene with tape to stop people from entering and disturbing the evidence.

If a piece of evidence has been removed for analysis, the forensic experts leave a number to show where it was found.

cordon off   to tape off and guard an area

The forensics team

Once a major crime has been discovered, the scene is soon filled with people dressed in white suits and masks. Each of these forensics experts has a special job to do.

Some of the experts take photos or videos to record the crime scene exactly as they found it. Others collect evidence. This could range from clothing to fingerprints, blood, scraps of paper and fabric, and even tiny fibres on the floor or walls.

The forensic photographer takes many photos from different angles at the crime scene.

contaminating   making something impure by adding a polluting substance

Patient and sharp eyed

The most important skills for the forensic experts are patience and careful observation. It can take hours, days or even weeks to collect all of the evidence at a crime scene.

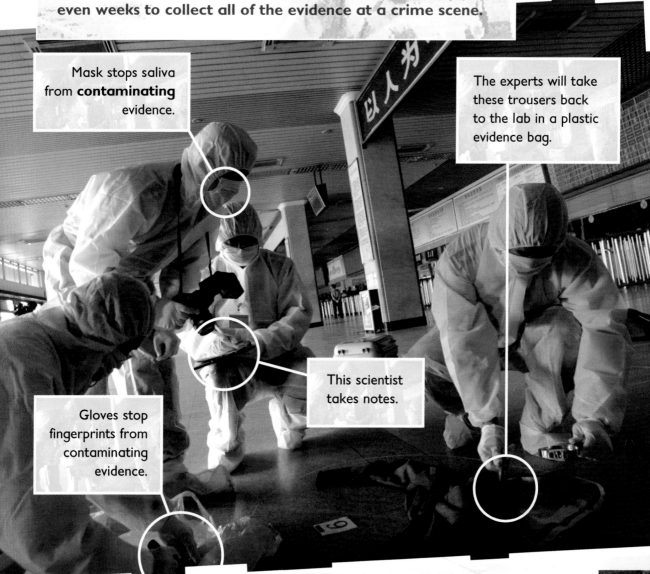

Mask stops saliva from **contaminating** evidence.

The experts will take these trousers back to the lab in a plastic evidence bag.

This scientist takes notes.

Gloves stop fingerprints from contaminating evidence.

These forensic experts in China are training to deal with bombings. They search for chemical evidence after an explosion.

Breaking and entering

Imagine being a forensics expert who has been called to the scene of a big robbery. One of the first things the police will want to know is how the robbers got in. The thieves may have broken in or had help from people inside.

Investigators look for a variety of clues. Some are simple. If there is glass under a broken window inside the building, the window must have been broken from the outside. The experts also examine locks and alarms to see if they have been damaged.

This robber smashed the glass door of a house using a hammer and reached in to unlock the door from the inside.

Quick get-away

Banks are protected by alarms and cameras. Once inside a bank, the robbers have only a few minutes to grab the money before the police arrive.

Photographers taking pictures of a tunnel after a bank robbery in Brazil. Thieves dug the 80-m (260-ft) tunnel under the neighbouring houses.

The tunnel was roughly 70 cm (2.3 ft) square and had its own lighting system.

The tunnel was 4 m (13 ft) deep and came up under the bank.

The thieves had to break through steel-reinforced concrete to break into the bank.

Sticky fingers

A forensics expert's main job is to find information that can help the police to identify the criminals. One of the best ways to do this is to find fingerprints.

Everyone's fingerprints are unique – unlike anybody else's. If criminals have touched objects at the crime scene, the police can use the fingerprints to prove the **culprits** were there.

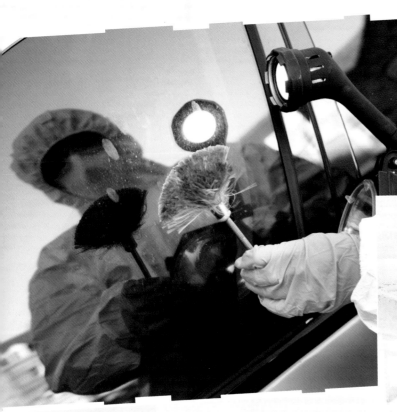

This forensics officer wipes dust over the car window so the fingerprints show up.

Fingerprint fraudsters

Some criminals used to go to great lengths to cover up their fingerprints. A few even had skin **grafted** on to their fingertips from elsewhere on their body.

culprits people who have done something wrong

Of course, fingerprints can come from innocent people as well as criminals. The forensic experts take fingerprints from everyone who might have left some at the crime scene: the people who work there, regular visitors, the cleaners, and so on. Any fingerprints that don't belong to these people might have come from the criminals.

This is a tented arch.

These are whorl patterns.

This is an arch with a loop above it.

Loops form the commonest pattern.

Fingerprints are made up of different patterns. This computer illustration shows coloured fingerprints.

grafted   moved from one part of the body to another using surgery

DNA fingerprints

Fingerprints are not the only way to identify criminals. DNA can also be used. Almost everyone has unique DNA.

When DNA is analysed, it forms patterns. Can you see which suspect's DNA matches the DNA at the crime scene in this simplified diagram?

Our bodies are made up of around 10 trillion cells. Nearly every one of these cells contains tightly coiled DNA in the centre.

A criminal may leave hairs, skin cells or tiny drops of blood at the crime scene. Each of these contains DNA. Forensic experts can analyse them to find the criminal's **DNA fingerprint**. The DNA fingerprint can be compared to DNA samples from suspects.

DNA at crime scene	Jeff	Tom	Anna	Kim

A forensic scientist takes a sample from a suspect's mouth to collect cells for DNA fingerprinting.

DNA fingerprint   the unique pattern formed from pieces of DNA

*This computer illustration shows a **molecule** of DNA, some DNA sequences and DNA fingerprints.*

Code for life

DNA is the instruction book for all living things. It contains the codes that determine how you grow, how you look, and many other things too. Apart from identical twins, no two people have the same **DNA**.

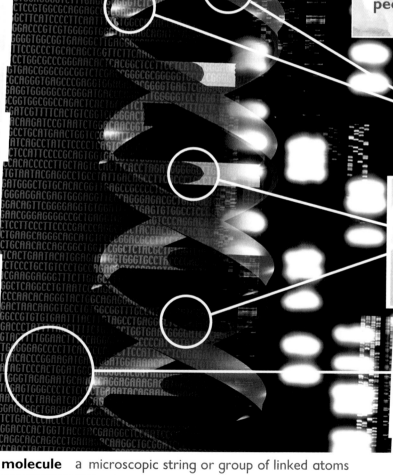

DNA is made up of two spirals.

Linking these two spirals are four chemicals (shown coloured blue, yellow, red and green) that form pairs.

The sequence of these chemicals is the genetic code.

molecule a microscopic string or group of linked atoms

Explosive evidence

Having a blast

Make your own mini explosion. Drop a chewy mint sweet into a glass of cola. Lots of gas is produced very quickly, and the cola quickly bubbles out of control like a little volcano. A real explosion is the same – but much, much bigger and faster!

Some of the clues a forensic expert gathers might not lead straight to the criminal. Yet they can still help the police to track down their target.

After an explosion, for example, forensic experts may find traces of the **detonator**. They may be able to tell the police what kind of detonator set off the explosion. The police compare it to the types of detonator used by different criminal groups. This will help them to work out which group carried out the crime, and may lead them to the criminals.

These are different kinds of explosives, including semtex (green) and TNT (brown).

detonator   device used to set off an explosion

A forensic expert collects evidence at the scene of a bomb explosion.

Explosives release huge amounts of gas very quickly. They cause an intense jolt, lots of noise and extreme heat.

A piece of the detonator has survived the blast.

Tiny traces of the explosive are left on the ground.

Strands of evidence

Even the tiniest piece of evidence can help the police identify a criminal. A single hair, for example, will contain a robber's DNA. Strands of fibre can also provide clues.

At every crime scene there are tiny strands of fibre from clothes and other fabrics. Most of these are useless to the police, but one or two may have been left behind by a criminal. Forensic experts can often work out what the culprit was wearing. Later, the fibres can be matched to the person's clothes to show that he or she was at the crime scene.

These microscope images show close-ups of strands of fibre. They were found in a bathroom where a crime took place.

Finding fabrics

Forensic experts find tiny strands of fabric using **ultraviolet (UV)** and **infra-red lights** and even vacuum cleaners!

infra-red light   light at the red end of the spectrum (the colours that make up light)

16

To understand how forensic experts work, try collecting strands of fibre from clothes and furniture in your home.

Using tweezers, place each strand in a separate evidence bag. Look at the fibres with a magnifying glass or microscope. Compare them to fibres from your family's clothes. Who has been in your room? Forensic experts work in this way to try to find evidence linked to a suspect.

These forensic scientists use UV light to find strands of fibre on these trousers.

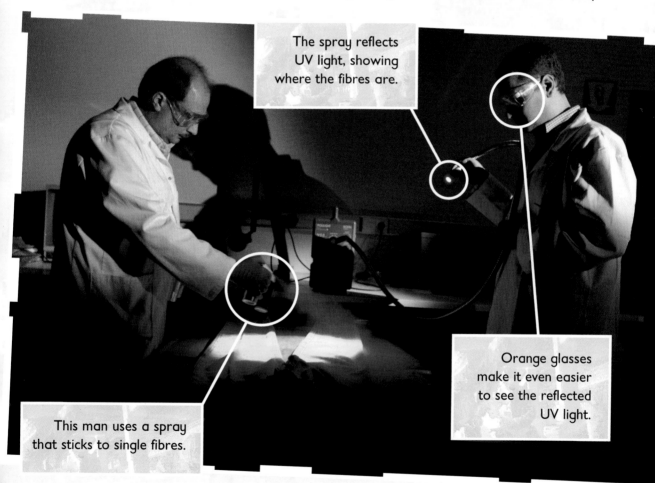

The spray reflects UV light, showing where the fibres are.

Orange glasses make it even easier to see the reflected UV light.

This man uses a spray that sticks to single fibres.

ultraviolet (UV) light   light at the blue end of the spectrum

Trails and tracks

Near many crime scenes, tyre tracks and footprints are left in soft soil or mud. These can provide valuable clues for a forensic investigator.

A forensics officer holds the plaster cast of a footprint found at the scene of a crime.

A forensic expert collects evidence from a car tyre.

Make a footprint mould

Make a running and walking footprint in soft soil. Pour liquid **plaster of Paris** into both types of footprint and let the liquid set. Carefully remove the moulds. Do they look different?

WARNING! You MUST ask an adult to help you with this activity.

plaster of Paris   a white powder that is mixed with water to make a paste that sets hard

Forensic experts take lots of photographs and make moulds from the footprints and tyre tracks. From footprints, they can work out the likely height and weight of the person. Soil from the crime scene will be in the tread of the criminal's car tyres and shoes. Experts examine the car and shoes of the suspects to look for a match.

The tracks show the direction in which the car was moving.

The tyre tracks show the type of car and the tyres it has.

The footprints show the size of the owner's feet and the type of shoes he or she was wearing.

Written evidence

Most people's handwriting is unique. Expert investigators looking at several different examples of handwriting can usually say whether they were all written by the same person or not.

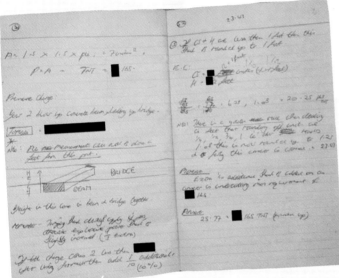

This means handwriting samples can often be used as evidence. Forensic handwriting experts can show that a ransom demand, or a note on how to disable an alarm system, was written by a particular person — even if he or she denies it.

These notes are about preparing and placing explosives. Experts analysed them and proved they had been written by Dhiren Barot. He was sent to prison for terrorism.

Invisible writing

If the suspect writes on a notepad, the writing will leave an imprint on the sheet underneath the note. Forensic experts can see these imprints using a special machine. It charges the paper with **static electricity** and makes black powder stick to the imprint.

static electricity the electrical charge produced by friction

Forensic experts also search for invisible evidence on written notes. They may find the criminal's fingerprints, DNA from skin cells or DNA from saliva if the person licked an envelope to send a letter.

This forensic scientist looks for fingerprints to find out who touched the letter.

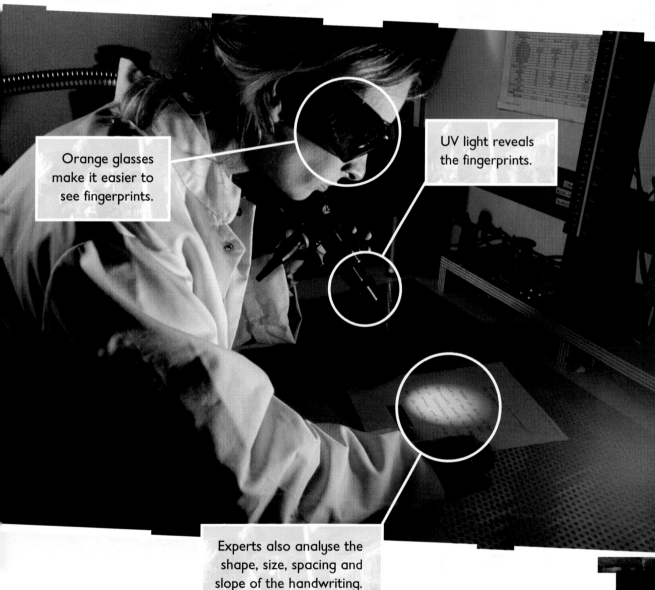

Orange glasses make it easier to see fingerprints.

UV light reveals the fingerprints.

Experts also analyse the shape, size, spacing and slope of the handwriting.

Ink clues

Even if it cannot be read, a tiny scrap of paper from a crime scene might provide investigators with an important clue.

Colours in ink

Pens have different inks that give them their colour. Using **chromatography**, forensic experts can separate these inks to make an individual pattern. Then they can compare the ink in a handwritten note with ink from pens in the suspect's home.

With paper chromatography, you can see how different inks separate into the pigments (substances used as colouring) that make them up.

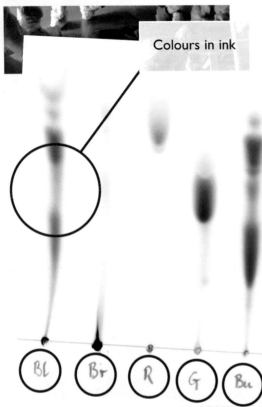

From left to right: black, brown, red, green, blue, orange.

Try out chromatography

Cut out five strips of kitchen roll. Using different felt tips, make a spot 1 cm (1/2 inch) from the bottom of each strip. Stick each strip to a piece of straight wire. Dip the end of each strip in water. The water rises up the strip and separates the pigments.

chromatography   separation of a substance into separate parts

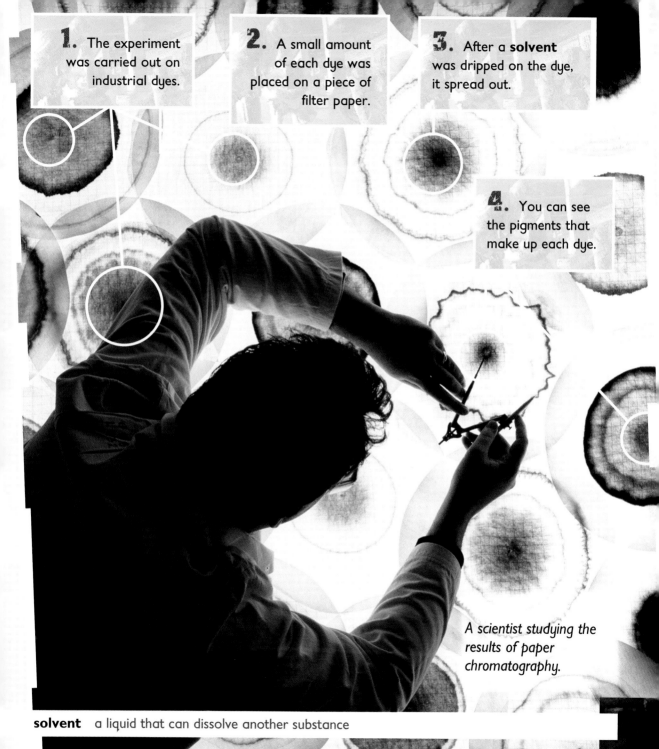

1. The experiment was carried out on industrial dyes.

2. A small amount of each dye was placed on a piece of filter paper.

3. After a **solvent** was dripped on the dye, it spread out.

4. You can see the pigments that make up each dye.

A scientist studying the results of paper chromatography.

solvent a liquid that can dissolve another substance

23

Magnificent microscopes

Microscopes are one of a forensic investigator's main tools. Almost everything that is brought back to a forensic lab is examined, a tiny piece at a time, using a microscope.

The **lenses** in a microscope allow forensic experts to find tiny pieces of evidence that are invisible to the naked eye. They might see minute strands of fabric from the culprit's clothes. If the suspect has carried explosives, tiny particles may have become caught in the fabric. Forensic scientists can see them with a microscope.

When a weapon is fired, smoke from the burning of the gunpowder surrounds the hand of the shooter. Tiny amounts of powder are left on the hand. This means that a forensic expert can work out if a person has fired a gun.

Microscopic

An electron microscope can magnify tiny things 2 million times, and can even show the surface of individual bacteria cells. These are so small that 1,000 of them could fit end-to-end on a pinhead!

lenses specially shaped pieces of glass or plastic that can bend and focus light to magnify objects

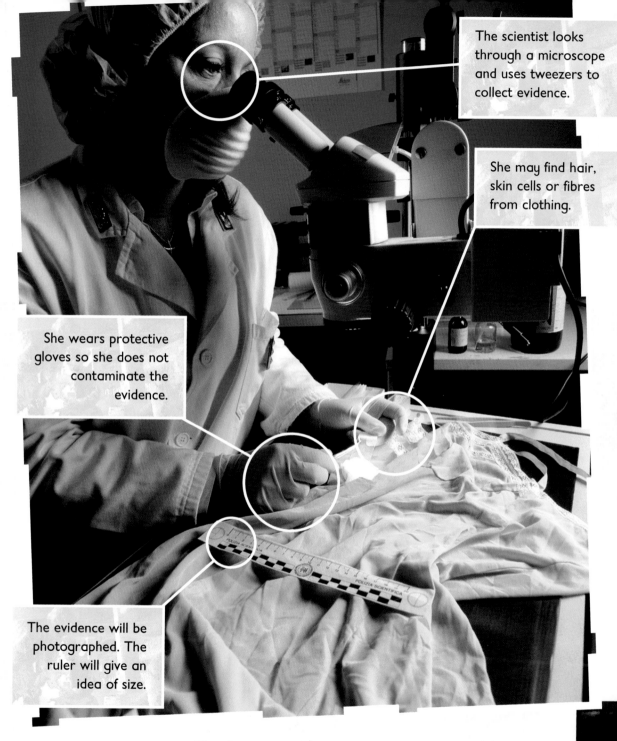

The scientist looks through a microscope and uses tweezers to collect evidence.

She may find hair, skin cells or fibres from clothing.

She wears protective gloves so she does not contaminate the evidence.

The evidence will be photographed. The ruler will give an idea of size.

This forensic scientist examines a dress from a crime scene.

Caught on camera

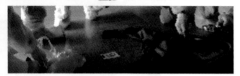

Crime scene investigators sometimes get help from **CCTV** cameras. If they're lucky, the cameras might even have filmed the criminal's face.

CCTV cameras work 24 hours a day, filming important places and areas where crime is likely to occur. Modern cameras can record what happens in great detail. Some can film in complete darkness using infra-red light.

This CCTV camera scans the cafeteria at a high school in the USA.

The streets have eyes

In these countries, people are most watched by **CCTV** and other **surveillance** forms: the UK, Singapore, Malaysia, Russia and China.

CCTV closed circuit television, which continually videos an area to protect it from crime

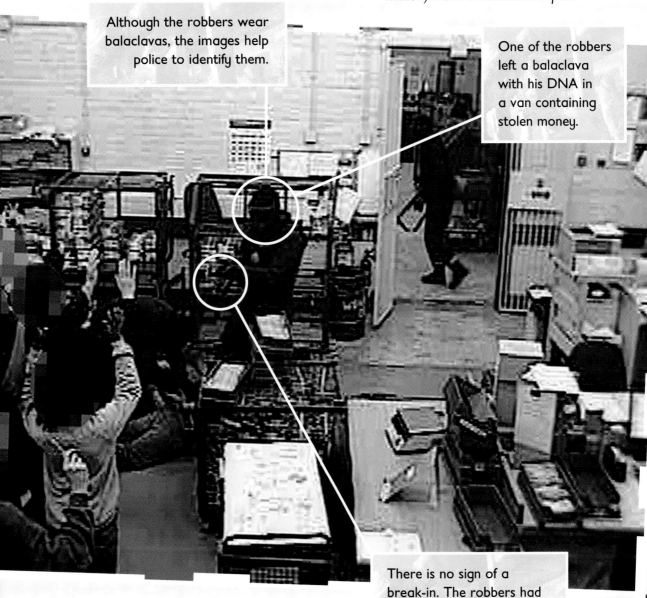

After a crime, the police and forensic experts examine the CCTV recordings to look for evidence.

This is CCTV footage of the UK's biggest armed robbery, in southern England in 2006. The robbers stole more than £53 million (US $105 million) from a Securitas depot.

Although the robbers wear balaclavas, the images help police to identify them.

One of the robbers left a balaclava with his DNA in a van containing stolen money.

There is no sign of a break-in. The robbers had forced the staff at gunpoint to open the depot.

surveillance watching a place where crime may occur

27

The evidence puzzle

DNA evidence used to convict Murdoch.

Forensic science can provide crucial evidence to help the police to capture criminals.

By using DNA fingerprinting and analysing substances found at the crime scene, the police can be nearly certain they have caught the right person. Yet they do not rely on science alone. They also use other information, such as **eyewitness** statements and databases with details of known criminals.

International check-in

Australian Bradley John Murdoch (centre) was found guilty of murdering British tourist Peter Falconio in 2001. Forensic scientists had found his DNA fingerprint at the crime scene.

DNA tricks

Some criminals have tried to beat the DNA experts. In 1992 Dr John Schneeberger committed a crime, but police could not match his DNA to the DNA found at the crime scene. To fool the testers he had surgically inserted a pipe filled with another man's blood into his arm.

eyewitness person who sees something happen

28

Sometimes criminals even provide evidence against themselves. Hidden in the memories of their computers are emails and other information proving they took part in a crime. Police often take the computers of suspects away to analyze this stored information.

A police officer removes a computer from the home of a murder suspect.

The police will examine the files on this computer's hard drive for clues that might help them to find the killer.

Glossary

CCTV closed circuit television, which continually videos an area to protect it from crime

chromatography separation of a substance into separate parts

contaminating making something impure by adding a polluting substance

cordon off to tape off and guard an area

culprits people who have done something wrong

detonator device used to set off an explosion

DNA fingerprint the unique pattern formed from pieces of DNA

eyewitness person who sees something happen

grafted moved from one part of the body to another using surgery

infra-red light light at the red end of the spectrum (the colours that make up light)

lenses specially shaped pieces of glass or plastic that can bend and focus light to magnify objects

molecule a microscopic string or group of linked atoms

plaster of Paris a white powder that is mixed with water to make a paste that sets hard

solvent a liquid that can dissolve another substance

static electricity the electrical charge produced by friction

surveillance watching a place where crime may occur

ultraviolet (UV) light light at the blue end of the spectrum

Further information

Books

Crime Scene Detective: Using Science and Critical Thinking to Solve Crimes by Karen Schulz (Dorling Kindersley, 2007)
This book challenges you to observe carefully, organize and record data, think critically and conduct simple tests to solve crimes.

Crime Scene Detective: Become a Forensics Super Sleuth, with Do-It-Yourself Activities by Carey Scott (Dorling Kindersley, 2007)
Activities to help you to become a super-sleuth.

Crime Scene Investigations: Real-Life Science Activities for the Elementary Grades by Pam Walker and Elaine Wood (Jossey Bass, 2007)
Neat tricks and simple techniques for careful observation and the collection of evidence.

Eyewitness: Forensic Science by Chris Cooper (Dorling Kindersley, 2008)
Discover the ground-breaking methods scientists use to solve crimes. Includes CD-ROM and charts.

Forensic Science by Alex Frith (Usborne Publishing Ltd, 2007)
Information about the science and methods that forensic experts use to collect evidence.

Forensics *(Kingfisher Knowledge)* by Richard Platt (Kingfisher, 2008)
Discover how to read the signs left by a criminal, find the evidence and learn what goes on in the crime laboratory.

Investigating Murder Mysteries by Paul Dowswell (Heinemann, 2004)
About the forensic techniques used in murder investigations – includes case studies.

Investigating Thefts and Heists by Alex Woolf (Heinemann, 2004)
Discusses how some famous robbery cases were solved using forensic science.

Websites

http://homeschooling.gomilpitas.com/explore/crimescene.htm
Activities to show how science is used to solve crimes.

www.deathonline.net/decomposition/index.htm
Shows what happens when a living thing dies.

www.sciencenewsforkids.org/articles/20041215/Feature1.asp
Crime and the techniques that forensic experts use to collect evidence.

Index